MEETING
with
GOD

A DAILY GUIDE

Carolyn Nystrom

Harold Shaw Publishers
Wheaton, Illinois

ISBN 0-87788-524-9

Cover photo © 1991 by Robert McKendrick

Library of Congress Cataloging-in-Publication Data

Nystrom, Carolyn.
    Meeting with God : a daily guide / Carolyn Nystrom.
      p. cm.
    Includes index.
    ISBN 0-87788-524-9
    1. Bible—Study. 2. Devotional calendars. I. Title.
  BS1193.N97 1991
  220'.076—dc20   91-6747
                                       CIP

99 98 97 96 95 94 93 92 91

10 9 8 7 6 5 4 3 2 1

Contents

Before You Begin

A new interest in spiritual matters brews today. Authorities of all varieties tell us how to fully develop our inner selves: through meditation, "space music," special retreats.

But while this emphasis on spiritual awareness is new to the general public, it is not new to Christians. Throughout the centuries, Christians have been concerned about spiritual growth and health. New Age strategies for sorting out our lives raise red flags of caution for us (we must not idolize ourselves, and we must not fall captive to our feelings as the New Age advocates). Yet, when we turn to the traditional means of spiritual nurture, we face the same problems our parents and grandparents did.

"I'd like to have regular devotions with God, but I don't know what to do."

"Sometimes I read the Bible, close it, and can't remember one idea. I might as well have been reading the phone book."

"I want to pray, but I don't know how to begin. So I just sit awhile and wish I could think of something to say. Worse, I speak a prayer, of sorts, but I feel as if I'm conducting a monologue with myself."

Popular culture in the 1990s claims that the Bible isn't enough anymore, that we must empty ourselves of old perceptions of God and spirituality. But growing Christians know that the well-beaten paths of prayer, Bible study, and meaningful fellowship are still as appropriate for spiritual growth as they were centuries ago in the catacomb meetings of persecuted believers. These are the same disciplines Jesus depended on—much time alone with God in prayer and lifelong study of the Scriptures.

This interactive studyguide is designed to help you establish healthy habits of prayer, Bible study, and meditation. It gives passages for Bible reading, questions to help you study, and plenty of space for notes. It also includes ideas for prayer based on the passage you are studying and more space to make notes on what you are saying to God.

But if your devotional time ends when your prayer is finished and your Bible is closed, something basic is lacking. What God teaches you in your time alone with him should affect the way you think, what you do, and how you feel. Each study gives suggestions to help you think about the changes God wants you to make in your life. As you meet with God, you'll grow to be more like him.

How to Use This Book

Each of the ten chapters in this book deals with a major topic of the Christian life. It will take you several weeks to study each chapter, but if you complete the studies on schedule, you'll finish the guide in a year. By then you'll be well on your way to establishing good, consistent devotional habits. And you will have studied a substantial portion of the Bible in detail.

The questions in this guide are designed to help you discover the content and meaning of the Scripture passages and to apply their truths to your life. As is true of any new program or exercise, the beginning is fairly structured. By the end of the book, while there are still several weeks left to the year, the Bible studies are not written out; instead there are suggestions for studies you can put together on your own.

Use a modern translation of the Bible. It will help clarify some of the language of the older versions. Try reading the Bible aloud as you study. Hearing, saying, and seeing the words simultaneously will help you remember them. And you'll soon know if your mind starts to wander—you'll stop hearing yourself read.

Be sure to include time for both Bible study and prayer. God wants to speak to you through his Word, but he also wants you to talk to him. Try praying aloud, too. You'll be amazed at how this helps you concentrate. Besides, prayer is more real in your own thinking if you've actually *said it.* You'll find the Prayer Notebook (pp. 180-181) helpful for keeping track of requests and answers as you intercede for yourself and others.

As this two-way communication with God grows, you'll begin to look forward to your time with God and feel a void if you miss it. More important, you'll see changes in what you say and do. By then, you'll know that God's Word is transforming your life—that God is making you more and more into the image that he has designed for you alone, an image that reflects God himself.

ONE

Prayer: Talking and Listening

Elbows on closed Bible, I cried,
Say, God, are you there?
Knock, knock, I need you!
Do you hear me?
Talk to me.
Tell me what to do.
I've lost my way.
I can't hear you.
Say, God, are you there?
I waited for some flash of light,
A voice, a roar from God on high.
Instead I heard a gentle click,
a door unlatched
between the covers
of his Book.

We talk to God. God talks to us. Communication between God and his people is two-way. During these first two months, you can learn about this two-way talk and practice some new ways of keeping the communication lines open.

The five studies in this chapter are about five kinds of prayer: praise, petition, confession, intercession, and thanksgiving. Just in case that all sounds very technical, take a look at the introduction to each study. You'll likely discover you're already using those prayers. But the Bible study should help you pray more as God intends.

The four studies in the next chapter deal with ways God talks to us. You might be surprised to discover that he's been talking to you all along. But maybe you'll find a few new ways to listen.

These Scripture study passages are short, but the questions have many answers. Read each passage several times during the week, and keep digging to find more answers. Fill up the pages with what God is teaching you.

□ Week 1

Praise

You look at your schedule for the week and wonder how you can possibly make it through. On top of your usual hectic pace, you're scheduled to speak at two workshops.

You look up from your calendar and notice a scarlet cardinal perched on a snow-covered branch outside. It reminds you of God's care, even for sparrows, and you feel renewed.

Whispering a quick prayer of *praise,* you say, "God, you are faithful, and I love you."

Read 1 Samuel 1:1–2:10, 21.

DAY 1

1. Write what you think Hannah said when she prayed silently (1:13).

2. Read verses 1:8 and 1:18. What caused this change in Hannah?

DAY 2

3. In what ways did Hannah show love for her son?

4. Hannah worshiped with a prayer of praise. What did Hannah tell God of her feelings toward him (2:1)?

DAY 3

5. How did Hannah describe God? Begin each description with "God is . . . " (2:2-3).

6. Find three contrasts in verses 4 and 5. What do these tell of God's character?

DAY 4

7. List Hannah's account of God's actions (2:6-9).

8. What does she say that God will do in the future (2:10)?

DAY 5

9. Prayers of praise are like giving God a compliment. We tell him about the qualities of himself that we appreciate. Make a list of good things God has done for you. Next to each item, write a "God is . . ." statement related to that gift. Today begin your prayer time with a note of praise from this list.

What God has done	*God is . . .*
Example: God gave me new friends when we moved to this new city.	God knows I need friends. He cares about the way I feel. God is a giver.
_____	_____
_____	_____
_____	_____
_____	_____

□ Week 2

Petition

You're coming home from a late meeting, and the road is far more slippery than when you left. It's hard to see through the snow. The car begins to swerve, and suddenly you see a telephone pole looming in front of you. You have time to gasp only, "Help Lord!" A prayer of *petition*—in its simplest form.

Read Isaiah 36–37.

DAY 1

1. What taunts did the Assyrian field commander use against the people of Judah (36:4-10)?

2. How did the commander undercut the confidence of the people (36:11-20)?

DAY 2

3. How did Hezekiah and his people respond to this threat from their enemy, Assyria (36:21–37:4)?

4. What reassurance did the prophet Isaiah offer (37:5-7)?

DAY 3

5. What did Hezekiah do with this new message from the king of Assyria (37:8-14)?

6. What praise did Hezekiah offer God in his prayer (37:15-16)?

7. What facts did he give God (37:18-19)?

8. What did he ask God for (37:17, 20)?

9. What reason did he give God for answering his prayer (37:20)?

DAY 4

10. What was God's response (37:21-38)?

DAY 5

11. Bring a problem to God today. Write the facts on paper. Spread it before the Lord as Hezekiah did his letter. Date your request. Then leave a space to write how and when God answers your prayer.

Date:
Problem:

Answer:

Date:

☐ Week 3

Confession

You blew it! It didn't seem so bad at the time, just a little lie and said with a smile. Someone might have even thought it was a joke. But it's mushroomed, and terrible consequences have resulted. Now you know it was all wrong from the beginning. You slip to your knees, bury your head in your arms, and *confess,* "God, I'm so sorry. I was wrong."

Read Luke 15:11-32.

DAY 1

1. Why do you think the young man's plan looked good to him at first?

2. What went wrong?

DAY 2

3. Study the young man's planned speech to his father in verses 17-19. What attitudes toward his father does this speech reflect?

4. What attitudes toward himself and his actions?

DAY 3

5. Do you think that the younger son's reception at home was more or less than he deserved? Why?

6. If you were given five minutes to defend the older brother's position, what points would you make?

DAY 4

7. If this story is a picture of God and his children when we sin, what does it reveal about the ingredients of confession?

About the way God responds to confession?

About the nature of forgiveness?

DAY 5

8. Are you ever plagued by a vague feeling of guilt about all sorts of things you've done in the past? God can heal those memories. Divide your past into three sections of time. One by one bring each section to God, confessing all your mistakes, failures, and sins of that time period. Trust him to enter your past and make you clean in his sight. Then read 1 John 1:9 to remind you of his forgiveness: "If we confess our sins, he is faithful and just and will forgive us our sins and purify us from all unrighteousness."

Age 0-12

Age 12-15

Age 15-present

□ Week 4

□ Week 4

Intercession

Your friend, Jim, is in an awful jam. His parents are getting a divorce. Neither his mom nor his dad wants him around. His grades have hit the skids. He's quit coming to church, and he says he might "drop out of life for a while." You're not sure what he means by that, but you do know he needs more help than you can give. You pray, "God, help Jim . . ." And so you *intercede* for your friend.

Every Day

This week, pray for a different person or group each day. Use the prayers listed below and insert the names you have chosen in the prayers as you read them to God.

Prayer	*Name*
Hebrews 13:20-21	_____
1 Thessalonians 5:23	_____
Philemon 4-7	_____
Ephesians 3:14-21	_____
Romans 15:13	_____
2 Corinthians 13:7-9	_____

Read Genesis 13:1-13 and 18:16-33.

DAY 1

1. Why did Abraham and Lot separate?

2. What reasons did Lot have for choosing the Sodom area?

DAY 2

3. Why did God tell Abraham that he was about to destroy Sodom?

4. What attitudes did Abraham show when he spoke to God?

DAY 3

5. What reasons did he give God for answering his request?

6. Was Abraham interceding for Sodom or for his nephew Lot?

DAY 4

7. What examples of Abraham's can you follow when you pray for someone else?

DAY 5

8. What can you know about God from this passage?

☐ Week 5

Thanksgiving

It's Saturday morning, bright, crisp, and clear. Autumn's skillful fingers have touched the fields and trees with gold. Even the air hints of gold dust suspended in sparkling liquid. You're free for the day— free in time and spirit. A morning walk turns your mind to God who thought it all up even though you can hardly take it in. You whisper, "Thank you, my Lord"—a prayer of *thanksgiving*.

Read Psalms 105–106, 136.

Preview this week's entire study, since it may require more time than usual, and you will need to budget your schedule accordingly.

DAY 1

1. All of these psalms praise God. Make notes about the characteristics of God that the psalmist appreciates.

Psalm 105:1-7

Psalm 106:1-5

Psalm 136

DAY 2

2. Outline Psalm 105.

3. How many times does the writer of Psalm 105 use the word *he* followed by a verb to show what God has done?

DAY 3

4. Why does the psalmist refer to God's steadfast love at the beginning and end of Psalm 106?

5. What reason does the psalmist give God for saving his nation (106:47)?

DAY 4

6. Both Psalm 105 and 106 recount the history of Israel. How are their emphases different?

7. Which works of God are added in Psalm 106 to what the psalmist already gave thanks for in Psalm 105?

DAY 5

8. Each verse of Psalm 136 has the same refrain. What is it?

9. Make a list on a separate sheet of paper of the works of God that make you thankful. Then think of a one-line refrain of praise. Write your own psalm of thanksgiving from this pattern.

My Psalm of Thanksgiving

T W O

How God Talks to Us

Is prayer merely an exercise in self-dialogue, a handy way of sorting out our own thoughts? Did God give us the gift of prayer simply so that we could pretend that "somebody up there" cares about us?

No. God doesn't leave us to pray alone, our prayers bouncing back at us from off the ceiling. God is a God who hears us, who loves us, and who allows us the unspeakable privilege of knowing him.

God reveals himself in many ways. He doesn't expect us to stumble through life's choices in a vacuum, doing only what feels best at the time and hoping a God far away will understand. Instead he gives us guidelines for choices, and these guidelines are rooted in his own perfect nature.

During the next four weeks you'll study four ways that God communicates with us. They include: the person of Jesus Christ, a personal encounter with God himself, circumstances, and Scripture.

No one prays alone. God hears and returns the conversation.

□ Week 6

Jesus Shows Us God's Will

When you were a child, did you ever wish for an older brother, one who would defend you, teach you, and introduce you to his friends? God talks to us in many ways. One of these is through the greatest older Brother ever—Jesus.

Read Hebrews 1.

DAY 1

1. How does God speak to us differently from the way he did to his people of Old Testament times?

2. List everything this passage says about God's Son.

DAY 2

3. What can you know about angels from this chapter?

4. How is Jesus superior to angels?

DAY 3

5. How does this passage show that Jesus is also God?

6. What does the life of Jesus tell you about the nature of God?

DAY 4

7. What have you learned from the teachings of Jesus?

DAY 5

8. Read Romans 8:29. In what ways can you see that God is making you more like his first-born?

9. List your activities for the coming week. What are some specific ways in which you can be more like Christ as you participate in these events?

□ Week 7

Encountering God

Do you ever wish that God would just sit down next to you and talk to you face-to-face as he did to Moses, Elijah, and the prophets? Then there would be no misunderstanding about whether God is leading you or your own thoughts are just adding to your confusion. God doesn't talk to us out loud now. Instead, the Holy Spirit lives inside us to help us know him. But he is the same God as in Old Testament times, and we can understand something of how he communicates with us by looking at how he talked to his people long ago.

Every Day

Sometimes we have to be quiet to understand what God is saying to us. This week, spend some of your devotional time each day being quiet before God. Empty your mind of other thoughts and concentrate on him. Let God reassure you of his presence. Let him bring understanding to what you have studied of his Word. Let him teach you to worship him.

Read 1 Kings 19.

DAY 1

1. Why was Jezebel angry at Elijah? (For details see 1 Kings 18.)

2. Why was Elijah discouraged?

DAY 2

3. How did God strengthen and protect Elijah?

4. How did God encourage him?

DAY 3

5. How did God illustrate his presence?

6. Which way did God choose to show himself to Elijah? Why do you think Elijah needed to know God in this way?

DAY 4

7. What did God tell Elijah?

8. How did Elijah change after meeting God?

DAY 5

9. What do verses 11 and 12 teach about the ways God speaks to his people?

10. Which way do you need to hear God speak? Why?

Circumstances

Do you sometimes look up after a long siege of things going wrong and wonder, "Is God trying to tell me something?" Or when everything is going great, do you say, "God must be with me?" Circumstances are not always an indication of God's leading, but they are one way that God helps us to know his will. Let's see how God used circumstances in Gideon's life.

Read Judges 6–7.

DAY 1

1. Why were the Midianites giving the Israelites so much trouble?

2. What reasons did Gideon have to doubt the angel's words?

3. What circumstances reassured Gideon (6:16-24)?

DAY 2

4. What was God's first step to defeat the Midianites (6:25-35)?

5. Try to imagine Gideon's feelings. When have you felt like this?

DAY 3

6. With all the enemies of Israel assembled at one spot, Gideon decided he needed even more evidence that God was with him. What signs did he receive this time (6:36-40)?

7. Why and how did God reduce Gideon's army from 32,000 to 300 (7:1-8)?

DAY 4

8. What new circumstances did God use to convince Gideon that he was still on the right track (7:9-15)?

9. What results of this battle showed that God continued to be with Gideon (7:19-25)?

DAY 5

10. Circumstances are not ironclad indications of God's will. But God's expectations of us are reasonable. He doesn't usually lead a D student to become a doctor. And he isn't likely to lead a gifted musician to stop his or her piano. Today, list areas in which you have been successful. Make another list of areas in which you have had consistent failure. Present both lists to God, and ask his guidance for where you should concentrate your efforts.

☐ Week 9
_____

The Bible

And now for the most reliable method of all by which God communicates with us: the Bible. This week study what the Bible has to say about itself. Each day read a different passage and answer the questions for that passage.

DAY 1

Read Psalm 1.

1. How does the writer of this passage feel about God's Word?

2. What responsibilities does the reader of God's Word have?

3. What blessings can one who studies and obeys God's Word expect?

4. If you believe and act on the teachings of this passage, what changes will you need to make?

DAY 2

Read 2 Timothy 3:16-17.

1. How does the writer of this passage feel about God's Word?

2. What powers does God's Word possess?

3. What responsibilities does the reader of God's Word have?

4. What blessings can one who studies and obeys God's Word expect?

5. If you believe and act on the teachings of this passage, what changes will you need to make?

DAY 3

Read Psalm 19:7-14.

1. How does the writer of this passage feel about God's Word?

2. What powers does God's Word possess?

3. What responsibilities does the reader of God's Word have?

4. What blessings can one who studies and obeys God's Word expect?

5. If you believe and act on the teachings of this passage, what changes will you need to make?

DAY 4

Read Hebrews 4:12.

1. How does the writer of this verse feel about God's Word?

2. What powers does God's Word possess?

3. What responsibilities does the reader of God's Word have?

4. What blessings can one who studies and obeys God's Word expect?

5. If you believe and act on the teachings of this verse, what changes will you need to make?

DAY 5

Read Psalm 119:97-112.

1. How does the writer of this passage feel about God's Word?

2. What powers does God's Word possess?

3. What responsibilities does the reader of God's Word have?

4. What blessings can one who studies and obeys God's Word expect?

5. If you believe and act on the teachings of this passage, what changes will you need to make?

6. God will never, never, never lead you to do something that is against the teachings of Scripture—not by circumstances, not by an inner feeling, not by the advice of your friends. What plan of action can you form to show God that you care about what he has to say to you through his Book?

T H R E E

And the Walls Came Tumbling Down

*Once
there was a barrier between
God and man.
Jesus ripped it
top to bottom
and thus he trampled
underfoot
the walls men build
between themselves.*

Walls. We build them. We stumble over them. We hide behind them. They become our prisons. And God doesn't want his people behind bars. Each Scripture passage in this chapter and the next speaks of walls. Read the passage and questions for the week several times. Schedule your time to complete all the questions within the week. Study. Think through the questions. Most of the questions have several answers. See if you can find a few new ideas to record each time you read.

Pray. Ask God to reveal any barriers between himself and you. Unconfessed sin can bring coldness to your fellowship with God. So can an unwillingness to obey him.

Then review your contacts with other people. Ask God to point out walls between you and them. (It doesn't matter who built the walls.) Pray for those people on the other side. Then seek his help in bringing the barriers to a crashing end.

□ Week 10

The Sin Barrier

Y ou've just returned from a noisy outdoor concert. Your ears are
still ringing from the sound. Your hair smells like a burnt rope. You've
heard so many obscenities from the crowd in the past two hours that
they sound almost natural. On the way home, you flip on the radio
and catch a newscast full of rape, murder, and war. You wonder, "How
can dirty, ugly, sinful humankind approach a holy God?"

Read how God circumvented this barrier in the Old Testament.

Read Exodus 26:31-37 and Leviticus 16.

DAY 1

1. Draw a picture of what is described in the Exodus passage.

2. What was the purpose of the veil?

DAY 2

3. When and under what conditions was the high priest to enter the holy place within the veil (see Leviticus 16)?

4. What reasons does God give for these restrictions?

DAY 3

5. What was the purpose of the bull (16:11-14)?

6. What was the purpose of the goat used for a sin offering (16:15-19)?

7. What function did the scapegoat serve (16:20-22)?

DAY 4

8. How was the veil a barrier between God and people?

9. How was it also a link?

DAY 5

10. What can you know about the nature of God from these passages?

Pray, worshiping him for these qualities.

☐ Week 11

Jesus Breaks the Barrier

Easter bunnies made of sugar; Easter clothes, more fancy than you like; Easter wicker baskets; Easter marshmallow chickens, Easter cellophane grass; "Easter Parade" blaring from the loudspeaker. The department store is geared up for the next big holiday.

Somewhere you notice a cross, but even that is candy-coated, not at all resembling jagged wood and rugged spikes, anguish, blood, torturously slow death.

So Easter celebrates Christ's death and resurrection, or are they thinking only that God died?

Read Matthew 26–28.

DAY 1

1. What indications are there that Jesus knew he would die (26:1-45)? List the verses as well.

2. What shows that this whole process was emotionally, spiritually, and physically painful to him (26:36-45)?

DAY 2

3. How is Christ's blood like the scapegoat of Leviticus 16?

4. What supernatural phenomena accompanied his death (27:50-54)?

5. In view of its Old Testament purpose and use, what is the significance of the torn temple veil? (See Exodus 26:31-37.)

DAY 3

6. How is the relationship between God and people different because of Christ's death and resurrection?

DAY 4

7. What does it mean to you that you can, by prayer, come into the presence of a holy God through Jesus' name?

DAY 5

8. What do you know of Jesus from these chapters in Matthew?

Pray, thanking God for these characteristics.

☐ Week 12

Jesus, Our High Priest

"**A**nd finally, beloved congregation . . ." You sigh as the pastor winds up his message. You have been daydreaming during the sermon in spite of your best intentions. You straighten your back, determined at least to tune in now. And so you hear the end of what must have been a substantial message: "We see Christ, the Great High Priest, taking the place of the entire old system of priesthood and at the same time becoming the blood sacrifice necessary for an atonement of sin—not just for one year but for all people and forever. The shredded temple veil leaves naked before us the Mercy Seat, where we can come face-to-face with a holy God. Though we may cover our own eyes in shame because of our sin, God receives us in love through his Son."

Read Hebrews 7:22–10:25.

DAY 1

1. How is Jesus like the Old Testament high priests?

2. How is he different?

3. List the promises of the new covenant (8:10-12).

DAY 2

4. What does it mean to you to know that God says, "I will be your God"?

5. In what ways was the holiness of God emphasized by the Old Testament method of sacrifice (9:1-10)?

6. What did it cost Jesus to become the High Priest forever (9:11-15)?

DAY 3

7. Have you accepted Christ's gift that breaks down the wall between you and God and offers permanent forgiveness for your sins?
   If yes, thank him again for this gift.
   If not, would you like to receive him? Here's how:
   a. Confess to him that you have sinned.
   b. Tell him that you accept his gift of new life now.
   c. Promise that you will try as hard as you can, with his help, to obey him in everything.
   d. Christ has already promised to receive you (John 6:37).

DAY 4

8. What does God ask us to do as a result of Christ's work for us (10:19-25)?

9. In which of these areas do you need to improve? What steps can you take to improve?

DAY 5

10. Who needs your encouragement this week?

11. What will you do for him or her? When?

F O U R

People Pens

Farm yards provide a graphic picture of separation. The goats graze in their own grass pasture, with a sturdy fence separating them from the yard. The fence keeps them from eating a pair of jeans off the line, which they like as much as grass.

Pigs wallow in their own pens placed downwind from the farm house. (Pigs smell best in the form of bacon.)

The cows amble through their wide barbwired meadow. They don't mix well with pigs and are apt to trample chickens.

And chickens? They peck away in a small enclosed dirt yard with chicken wire high enough to keep them from flying over and annoying any animal not equally airborne. Each animal in its own fenced-in area—a perfectly appropriate arrangement for farm animals.

And people, even God's people, may industriously build invisible pens around themselves: for protection, for convenience, for privacy, for safety. Their pens say, "My space is for me and my own kind—the rest of you stay out!"

But when Jesus, by his death, ripped the temple veil—a symbolic barrier between God and us—he also trampled underfoot the walls we build between ourselves. During the next six weeks you will look at six different settings where people try to isolate themselves. And six Scripture studies will encourage you to stay out of those "people pens."

☐ Week 13

Cultural Differences

A letter arrives from unpredictable Cousin Sara, missionary to Indians in mountainous Columbia. She's coming home on furlough. This time there's a new wrinkle in her every-four-years' visit. She's bringing a family of Indians with her—mother, father, and four small children. She writes, "Don't worry about beds, they're all used to sleeping in one bed or hammock, whichever is available. Only plan two meals a day. We can't upset their digestive systems. Please try to have some coarse whole-grain foods. You may have to explain bathroom procedures. They've never used one before." (You eye the new carpet in your living room.) "And by the way, they speak little English but are very receptive to the gospel in their own tongue." (You don't happen to speak their language.) "And don't worry," she adds, "we won't stay long." (Long? You don't know if you're even up to an overnight stay.)

Read Acts 10:1–11:26.

DAY 1

1. What were the cross-cultural hurdles Peter had to make to go to Cornelius (10:9-14, 27-29)?

2. Why was Cornelius fertile ground for the gospel?

DAY 2

3. What are the indications that Cornelius was willing to be taught by Peter?

4. What do you think made it possible for Peter, a Jew, and Cornelius, a Gentile, to talk and listen to each other?

DAY 3

5. What information did Peter give Cornelius?

6. What do you think was his most important point? Why?

DAY 4

7. When Peter defended his actions, what authority did he use?

8. How did God use Barnabas to build on what Peter had learned?

DAY 5

9. Maybe it's not primitive Indians on the other side of your barrier. But what about a foreign-born coworker, or someone whose Christian doctrine is so different from yours that it hardly seems like the same faith? Or maybe your family is thinking of taking in a troubled foster child. Who is the "Cornelius" in your life?

What can you do to show him or her that Jesus Christ is "Lord of all"?

□ Week 14

The Body of Christ

"**M**r. Moderator, I'd like to speak against the motion that we pay the church organist."

The organist is not present at the annual church business meeting, but his wife is. She sits motionless and looks straight ahead.

"I think it would set a precedent we don't want to follow. Sure, Matt is talented; we could never pay him what he's worth. But we have talented Sunday school teachers, and a talented librarian, and a talented superintendent. We even have a talented church treasurer. But we don't pay any of them—and we shouldn't. We shouldn't pay a church organist either."

The church business meeting staggers on. First one side and then the other addressing what at first appeared to be a minor issue. Before it is over, two families (one from each side) have resolved to leave the church.

And for the church, the model of Christian unity—so much so that Paul calls it "the body (singular) of Christ"—something has gone crazily awry.

Read Ephesians 4:1-16.

DAY 1

1. Make a list of the ways in which we are "one" (4-6).

2. What gifts did Jesus give (8-11)?

3. For what purposes were the gifts given?

DAY 2

4. Who does the "works of service" (12)?

5. Why should we become spiritually mature (13-16)?

DAY 3

6. From your own experience, give some examples of speaking the truth *without* love.

Give some examples of speaking the truth *in* love.

DAY 4

7. How is your church acting like one body with Christ as the head?

8. What gifts (ability or service) should you contribute to this body?

9. How can you work toward overcoming barriers within your church?

DAY 5

10. Think of one person in your church with whom you do not work well (it might be someone much older or younger than you). Pray for this person.

This week, take one positive step toward working together as part of the body of Christ. What do you plan that step to be?

☐ Week 15

Economic Barriers

Where do you live, right side of the tracks or wrong? How about your race—majority or minority? When you choose friends, what do you look for? Probably you look for people mostly like yourself. It's easier to feel comfortable with them. But how do you feel about those who are of a different race, a different social status, those who can't match you dollar for dollar—or those whom you can't match? How do you treat them?

Read Philemon.

DAY 1

1. Think of one person that verses 4-7 describe. Write the prayer using his or her name.

Now pray it.

DAY 2

2. What were the social, class, and economic differences between Paul, Philemon, and Onesimus?

DAY 3

3. How had the status of Onesimus changed since he became a believer? How was it the same?

4. To what extent was Paul willing to go to bat for him?

DAY 4

5. What changes from the usual master-slave relationship was Paul requesting? (See also Ephesians 6:5-9.)

DAY 5

6. Think of one Christian that you have trouble loving because of social, racial, or economic differences. What can you do to treat that person as a "beloved brother or sister"?

☐ Week 16

Family Problems

There go Mr. and Mrs. Taylor. Their family is such a model that their backyard fruit tree must grow homemade apple pie. Mrs. T. has a ready smile that's not phony. Mr. T. listens appreciatively to his wife, and a quick caress isn't unusual. Yet he speaks with authority when it's his turn. Paul T., age 12, is the only kid in church who isn't afraid to pray out loud in an adult prayer service. Lynn T., age 10, acts as if she really likes to look after Craig, who is 2. She plays with him constantly. When Craig takes turns sitting on laps, each family member acts like Craig is doing him a favor. Sue T., who is 16, has a Bible study at her high school, and lots of kids think the Bible is O.K. just because Sue is wonderful. A college student once said, "Just knowing the Taylors reassures me that it's possible to get married and have things work out right."

You know deep down that any family, even the Taylors, can't be perfect. But still, there must be some system for making a family work. What is it?

Read Ephesians 5:15–6:4 every day.

DAY 1

1. What are four results of being filled with the Spirit (5:19-21)?

2. Name specific ways in which each member of your family can be "subject to one another out of reverence for Christ."

DAY 2

3. List the commands to a wife.

What reasons are given?

DAY 3

4. List the commands to a husband and father.

What reasons are given?

DAY 4

5. List the commands to children.

What reasons are given?

DAY 5

6. Which member of your family is hardest for you to get along with?

What changes toward that person should you make in order to follow these commands?

☐ Week 17

Personality Barriers

Ella is new at work. She is fat, ugly, has long, dark, stringy hair, talks loudly, and chews gum with her mouth open. Besides that, she doesn't practice "personal hygiene."

You know that Christ died for everyone, but surely he doesn't expect you to take someone like Ella under your wing. After all, if she were a Christian, she wouldn't even give his cause a good image!

Read Mark 10:46-52; Luke 19:1-10; John 4:4-42.

DAY 1

Try to answer the questions below for each of the three main characters.

1. What made each one appear to be an unsuitable follower of Jesus Christ?
Bartimaeus?

Zacchaeus?

Woman of Samaria?

2. What was the response of the people surrounding Jesus to each of these individuals?
Bartimaeus?

Zacchaeus?

Woman of Samaria?

DAY 2

3. What are the indications that each wanted to know Christ?
Bartimaeus?

Zacchaeus?

Woman of Samaria?

DAY 3

4. How did Christ respond to each?
Bartimaeus?

Zacchaeus?

Woman of Samaria?

DAY 4

5. What evidence is there that each was useful to him?
Bartimaeus?

Zacchaeus?

Woman of Samaria?

DAY 5

6. Think of one person who is naturally repulsive to you. Pray for that person. What is one act that you can do to show that person that Christ cares for him or her, and that you do, too?

☐ Week 18

Love Crumbles Barriers

Lord God,

There's this guy at work I just can't stand. On a Monday morning he can saunter through the plant whistling gospel tunes. Last week he stood next to my machine and just talked—on and on. The guy must be blind not to notice that I was working my tail off to make the piece rate. The last thing I need is a gabber to mess up my rhythm. (Maybe he doesn't need the money, but I do.)

And he carries this big grin around with him all day long. All this "Happy Joe" stuff has got the other workers tapping their heads behind his back.

Lord, I know I'm supposed to love this guy. (He's my Christian brother.) But I don't even like him.

Read 1 John 3:11–4:21; John 13:34-35.

DAY 1

1. In what ways does John tell us that God showed his love to us (1 John 4:9-11)?

2. What are some ways that we can imitate God's love in our relationships with others?

DAY 2

3. What reasons are given for showing love to each other (John 13:35; 1 John 4:11-12)?

DAY 3

4. What effect does the love of believers for each other have on nonbelievers (1 John 4:4-6; John 13:35)?

DAY 4

5. First John 3:18 speaks of love as more than words (and feelings)— as deeds. What can you do to be loving toward someone even if you don't *feel* loving? Think about a specific person.

DAY 5

6. How does knowing that another Christian loves you make it easier for you to love God?

God: Continuous Creator

void, darkness
God spoke.
light, land, water,
seed, beasts
Yet God wouldn't rest.
dust, a rib
man, woman
in his image
Breath of life from God—
shaped in his image
Alive!
And God rested.

God rested—after his period of initial creation—but not for long. The Scripture is full of God's creative activity. Sure, he made the world and all that's in it. (That includes the stars light years away and all those billions of stars beyond the ones we've discovered.) But when that was finished, God kept right on creating. He created people—not just the first two—but every tiny baby born since. David said in a prayer to God,

"For you created my inmost being;
you knit me together in my mother's womb" (Psalm 139:13).

The prophet Isaiah spins chapter after chapter, singing of God's overwhelming creative power. And the apostle Paul talks about God creating new life in the inner being of all who receive Jesus Christ. So God may have rested—but not for long. He keeps right on creating, even now.

During the next four weeks you'll study Scriptures that speak of God's continuous creativity. And after each study you'll find a suggestion for your own creative worship of our creative God.

☐ Week 19

First Creativity

Got an urge to create? Like to build, paint, write, sew, or sing? What causes you to read a story and think how you would have ended it differently? How do you think up new games to entertain the little kid next door? What makes you rearrange a room until the whole setting is one that says, "Now it's finally right (at least for this week)"? God started it way back "in the beginning."

Read Genesis 1–2.

DAY 1

1. What words and phrases are repeated in this passage? Make a list.

2. What do these tell you about God?

DAY 2

3. What words would you use to describe God's creativity?

4. How did God show that he cared about people?

DAY 3

5. In what ways did God make men and women different from the rest of his creation?

6. What difference does it make to you that you are created in God's image?

DAY 4

7. What do you need to change in order for your creativity to be more like the creativity of God?

8. Now tell God about this in a written prayer.

DAY 5

9. Read all of Genesis 1–2 again today. Meditate on the character of God as it is revealed in these chapters. Praise him, in prayer, for these qualities.

☐ Week 20

God Made Me

Ever feel like an unimportant blob in the midst of a vast universe, as if what you say and think doesn't matter? Maybe our whole world doesn't matter. It's just a "fleck of sand" anyway. Ever wonder if it makes any difference what you do or whether you exist at all? Will anyone know, or care, in a hundred years? Let's see it from God's perspective.

Read Psalm 139 every day.

DAY 1

1. How does the psalmist describe God's knowledge?

2. List the places the psalmist says you could expect to find God.

DAY 2

3. What does God know about you?

4. When did God begin to care about you?

DAY 3

5. God created a special gift of yourself for you. How can this change the way you feel about yourself?

DAY 4

6. Make a list of your characteristics, abilities, and personality traits.

Thank God for each one of these, and ask his help in using this creation of yourself to please him.

DAY 5

7. Psalm 139 is a beautiful prayer. It includes praise, worship, and much of the psalmist's inner feelings, as well as requests. Today write a prayer that has these elements. Then pray it to God.

□ Week 21

Our Creative God

What is God like? What does he do? Who is he? How can you describe God? What does your mind see when you say the word God? A God who created everything you know of is a pretty big God. Part of worship is recognizing God's characteristics and praising him for them. Biblical writers tried to describe God's creativity. Read one of the five listed chapters each day. Then write answers for that chapter.

Every Day

Page through a hymnal or songbook. Find a song that says what you would like to tell God. Then sing it to him each day this week.

DAY 1

Read Psalm 104.

1. What do the word pictures of verses 1-4 contribute to your feelings about God?

2. How do verses 5-9 help you see God's orderliness in something as devastating as the flood?

3. List everything God has made according to verses 10-26.

4. Why can the psalmist say in verse 24, "In wisdom you made them all"?

5. Notice the words in verse 27, "These all look to you." In what ways do verses 27-30 illustrate God's continuing creation?

6. Is your response to this psalm's description of God similar to verses 31-35? If so, read it as your prayer of praise to God.

DAY 2

Read Isaiah 42.

7. Verses 1-4 foretell the coming of Jesus. What do they reveal about his work?

8. How can a belief in God as Creator keep us from idolatry (5-9)?

9. What reasons do verses 10-17 show you for joining in the praise written here?

10. What steps did God take in verses 18-25 to keep his people from being blind and deaf to him?

11. Find one verse from Isaiah 42 that tells how great God is. Write it down.

DAY 3

Read Isaiah 43.

12. Which verses refer to God as Creator?

13. What do they say he created?

14. What motivation do you find here not to value anyone or anything more than God?

15. Find one verse from Isaiah 43 that tells how great God is. Write it here.

DAY 4

Read Isaiah 44.

16. From verses 1-5, what can you know of God's continuing creation?

17. Verses 6-23 are often referred to as one of the strongest statements against idolatry in all of Scripture. What do you find here that would turn you from other gods?

18. What do you find in the same verses that would turn your worship to the one true God?

19. How might God's ability to create (and re-create) inspire you to worship?

20. Find one verse from Isaiah 44 that tells how great God is. Write it here.

DAY 5

Read Isaiah 45.

21. What different forms does God's creative power take in this chapter?

22. Verses 9-13 begin with the words, "Woe to him who quarrels with his Maker." What reasons do these verses give for not quarreling with God?

23. Find as many repetitions as you can of the refrain, "I am the Lord and there is no other." List all that God compares himself to in order to show that he alone is God.

24. Verse 22 says, "Turn to me and be saved." Why might you want to turn to God as he is described in this chapter?

25. What would you hope this creative God would create in you?

26. Find one verse from Isaiah 45 that tells how great God is. Write it here.

☐ Week 22

New Creations in Christ

When God planned you, even before you were born, he knew that you would never be able to measure up to his standards. He knew that you would be subject to temper tantrums, feelings of jealousy, disobedience, selfishness, and all kinds of other sins. Therefore, he planned a way to make you new on the inside. Christ died for us, but his creative work on our behalf didn't end; it was only beginning. By his Spirit, he is continually making us beautiful new creations in his own image.

Every Day

Many of the people you see every day are in slavery to sin. Some would like to have the freedom of forgiveness and new life in Christ. God may already be preparing them to receive his free gift. Ask God to bring these people to your attention. This week pray each day for one of your acquaintances who does not know Christ. Some time during the week, worship God by presenting the gospel to that person. Write his or her name here:

Read Romans 6.

DAY 1

1. In what ways has Christ made it possible for us to be like him (1-11)?

DAY 2

2. What responsibilities do we have for our bodies (12-14)?

DAY 3

3. Contrast the effects of slavery to sin with the results of slavery to God. Make a list for each.

Slavery to Sin	*Slavery to God*
_____	_____
_____	_____
_____	_____
_____	_____
_____	_____
_____	_____

4. According to verse 23, what is the final result of each kind of slavery?

DAY 4

5. Write some specific effects of your sin.

DAY 5

6. Write specific effects of your acts of obedience to God.

7. Which kind of slavery do you prefer? Why?

S I X

God's Creative Creatures

How can we, human beings created by God and created again with new life in Christ, respond to this creative God—our Maker? Creatively, of course.

Here, too, Scripture gives us guidelines on how and when, and with what kind of help. The next four weeks' study outlines some of these ways.

First, new life in Christ grants us the indwelling presence of God the Holy Spirit. So we don't have to worry about whether our creative genes are as powerful as those of the next person. God created us the way he chose. And through the power of his Holy Spirit, we too can create.

But how can we create? Many, many ways. We'll look at three. We can worship God through creative use of our bodies, we can worship him through music, we can worship him through work. And our God who loves creativity receives it all.

☐ Week 23

God Makes Us Creative

When you look inside yourself, what do you see? No, not the X-ray, CAT scan version of bone, muscle, tendon. But what do you see of the inner you? The motives, feelings, thoughts, plans, desires. Ever wish you could turn the secret you inside out and send it to the cleaners?

God's offer of new life isn't just a paper promise. He offers to be that cleaner for you. God never says, "You clean up your life and then you may come to me." He says, "Come, I'll help you with the bath."

This week you'll study four Scriptures that will help you become more and more that new creation God envisioned of you when you first gave yourself to Jesus.

Every Day

As part of your creative worship this week, select a psalm that expresses what you feel. Write it in the space below. Then each day use it as a prayer.

DAY 1

Read 1 Samuel 9:25–10:13.

1. What signs did Samuel give Saul that God was working?

2. What did God do for Saul?

DAY 2

Read John 14:15-31.

3. What does Jesus promise us if we love him?

4. What does he expect from us?

5. How can you make yourself a better "home" (23) for God?

DAY 3

Read 2 Corinthians 5:14-21.

6. What does it mean to be a new creation in Christ?

DAY 4

Read Ephesians 4:17-32 today and tomorrow.

7. Make a list of the contrasts between the old nature and the new nature.

Old Nature	New Nature
_____	_____
_____	_____
_____	_____
_____	_____
_____	_____
_____	_____

DAY 5

8. How is God making you new? Make notes of some of these inside changes.

Thank God for these, and then ask him for help in specific areas that still need cleansing.

☐ Week 24

Creative Worship

God created our bodies, each one differently. We can use these bodies to express worship. Sometimes we pray with folded hands, as if placing them between his in commitment. We may bow our heads in submission or lift them to give attention to him. We may open our hands palms up to receive from him or to release ourselves to him. We can lift our hands, as if reaching toward God in worship.

Confession of sins seems more real if we kneel before him, a mighty and holy Lord. We cause our lips to speak to him and of him. We discipline our minds and spirits to think of him when we read his Word and pray. This week's Scripture passages speak of worshiping God with our bodies.

Every Day

Concentrate on prayer this week. As you pray, let your body reflect the words of your prayers. Give your body as a living sacrifice to God (Romans 12:1), and use it to worship him.

DAY 1

Read Romans 12:1-3.

Each day this week, read the suggested passage for the day. Then respond to the questions below with information and thoughts gleaned from that passage.

1. Find as many references as you can to the body, its parts, or position. How are these used in prayer or worship?

Body Part   *Reference*   *How Used*

_____   _____   _____
_____   _____   _____
_____   _____   _____
_____   _____   _____
_____   _____   _____

2. What characteristics of God inspire each of these gestures of worship?

3. How can this passage help your worship?

DAY 2

Read 1 Timothy 2:1-10.

1. Find as many references as you can to the body, its parts, or position. How are these used in prayer or worship?

Body Part   *Reference*   *How Used*

_____   _____   _____
_____   _____   _____
_____   _____   _____

2. What characteristics of God inspire each of these gestures of worship?

3. How can this passage help your worship?

DAY 3

Read Psalm 63.

1. Find as many references as you can to the body, its parts, or position. How are these used in prayer or worship?

Body Part	Reference	How Used
_____	_____	_____
_____	_____	_____
_____	_____	_____
_____	_____	_____
_____	_____	_____
_____	_____	_____

2. What characteristics of God inspire each of these gestures of worship?

3. How can this passage help your worship?

DAY 4

Read Psalm 95.

1. Find as many references as you can to the body, its parts, or position. How are these used in prayer or worship?

Body Part	Reference	How Used
_____	_____	_____
_____	_____	_____
_____	_____	_____
_____	_____	_____
_____	_____	_____
_____	_____	_____

2. What characteristics of God inspire each of these gestures of worship?

3. How can this passage help your worship?

DAY 5

Read Psalm 134.

1. Find as many references as you can to the body, its parts, or position. How are these used in prayer or worship?

Body Part	*Reference*	*How Used*
_____	_____	_____
_____	_____	_____

2. What characteristics of God inspire each of these gestures of worship?

3. How can this passage help your worship?

□ Week 25

A New Song

Do you sometimes wake up with a song buzzing through your head, almost as if it had been sitting there all night, waiting to burst out? Maybe it's a song you've heard, or maybe one you hardly remember, so you fill in your own words as you hum, or maybe it's a new song—all yours.

DAY 1

Read Psalm 33.

1. What can you imagine of the situations in which the psalmist sings a new song?

2. What praise does the psalmist offer God in his new song?

DAY 2

Read Psalm 144.

3. How does he describe God's power?

4. What does he request in his new song?

DAY 3

Read Psalm 149.

5. In what different ways are the people told to praise God?

DAY 4

Read Revelation 4–5.

6. In Revelation 4–5, the creatures of heaven praise Jesus with five new songs. Find their songs and write out the words.

7. What do these songs tell about Jesus?

8. What emotions are present in these chapters of Revelation?

9. Tell Jesus how it makes you feel to have him living in you. Make some notes here.

DAY 5

10. Pick out one of the new songs in these passages. Try to sense the mood of the words. Then make up a tune that fits the words and the mood. Use it as your new song to the Lord. If you're able to do so, write your tune on the staff paper below.

☐ Week 26

Creative Good Works

DAY 1

What did you do with your time last week? Disregard the time you spent with "have to" things like eating, sleeping, or work. How did you spend the rest of your time? Try making a list with an estimated number of hours for general categories like TV, sports, study, loafing, reading, and music. Need a category for "can't remember"? **Read Ephesians 2:8-10** to discover one of God's reasons for creating new life in you. Now go back over your schedule. How much of what you did last week could be called "good works"?

Things I Did	*How Much Time?*	*Good Works?*

DAY 2

Read Titus 1-3 for the next four days.

1. The book of Titus is a letter from Paul to the young pastor of the new churches on the island of Crete. In what general areas does Paul give advice to Titus?

2. What does Paul say that Titus ought to be teaching his congregations?

DAY 3

3. Find six references to good deeds in this book.

4. In view of Paul's broad range of teaching, what would you expect to be included in his definition of good deeds?

5. What part in a believer's life should good deeds have?

DAY 4

6. Paul says in Titus 2:14 that Christ's people ought to be "eager to do what is good." How can you cultivate an eagerness for good works?

7. What activities (that could be called good works) do you enjoy so much that you could become *eager* to do them?

DAY 5

8. Look again at last week's schedule. Put a check mark next to those activities that work toward making you a better person, helping someone else, or building up God's kingdom. Do you have some extra time left that you could have used for good deeds?

During the next few days, express your thanksgiving to God for new life by setting aside some time to work for him. Let these tasks be part of your worship. Record them below.

Date	*Time*	*Project*

SEVEN

History's Hieroglyphics

Those crazy Israeli!
On again
Off again.
Chosen by God,
yet fickle
Yell for God
in a jam.
Forget God
until the next crisis,
And wonder why
God doesn't bounce
around to rescue.
They've got God pegged
all wrong.
But who can peg God?
Can you?
Can I?
And if we could,
would we dare yell for help
at all?

Ancient Egyptians designed a special kind of writing—a writing in pictures called hieroglyphics. Remnants of this writing still turn up on ancient stones found at archaeological digs. In hieroglyphics, cryptic symbols stood for words whose meaning or sound resembled the picture. It was an ancient game of charades played out with stylus on stone. And it worked. In an era when written language was new, those picture symbols stuck in the mind. Reading and remembering went hand in hand.

History in the Bible carries some of that same advantage. We can read long convoluted lectures from an apostle or a prophet and get lost in the intricate logic. But history is a story. It has time and place and events and people: picture writing. It sticks in our minds.

For the next nine weeks you will study a quick overview of the history of God's people. The focus is primarily on worship, but it is a *history* of worship. How people did it right—and wrong. What happened when worship failed, or succeeded. And what kind of God is sovereign over all the universe, yet invites, even desires, worship from individual people.

You'll open with an experience of Isaiah, a prophet to ancient Judah. Astounding as it may seem, Isaiah saw God. And for him, worship was no problem. It came automatically.

After that you'll begin this picture of history appropriately in Genesis with Abraham, founder of God's chosen people. From there, you'll hop/skip, touching down at dramatic moments all the way to the apostle Paul's letter to his young friend Timothy nearly two thousand years later.

Enjoy your brief trip through history's hieroglyphics. Let its picture writing cling to your mind—and inspire you to worship.

☐ Week 27

God Is Holy

The country of Judah appeared to be prospering under King Uzziah. He had an army of 307,500 strong men, so neighboring countries treated them with respect. But the Judeans became proud. Who needed God when they had so much power of their own? So God sent Isaiah to warn his people. As if to give the prophet an extra push, God allowed him to see a glimpse of himself. Isaiah tells us what he saw in his sixth chapter.

If we are to worship God, we must know something of what he is like. What does it mean to say that God is holy? Read this chapter every day, and record a few new answers each time.

Read Isaiah 6.

DAY 1

1. Suppose you had stood in Isaiah's shoes during the events of verses 1-4. What would your five senses have revealed to you?

2. What qualities in God does this picture suggest?

DAY 2

3. How did the seraphim show honor to God?

4. What was Isaiah's reaction to this revelation of God's holiness?

DAY 3

5. How did God prepare Isaiah for his task of prophesying to the people of Judah?

6. What does the contrast of verses 5 and 8 tell you about the change in Isaiah?

DAY 4

7. What was going to be hard about Isaiah's job?

8. From the text finish this sentence about the future of Judah in as many ways as you can. "It will be so bad that . . ."

DAY 5

9. Write the song of the seraphim (3).

What does it tell you about God's nature, power, resources, and scope of dominion? (Look up *holy* in the dictionary.)

Close your eyes and meditate on this song. Worship God for the qualities that it brings to mind.

☐ Week 28

God's Covenant to Abraham

Organized worship started when God called a special group of people to be his own. He began with Abraham, a seventy-five-year-old semi-nomad from Ur. Ur was a city-kingdom of an early Babylonian empire. The moon-god "Sin" was its people's chief god. First God called Abraham to travel 600 miles to Haran with relatives, and there his father, Terah, died. Then God called him even farther away from friends and family and those who worshiped false gods.

Although God didn't let Abraham know where he was going, he did reassure him with a covenant. Many times when Abraham was in a difficult situation, God gave his promises again.

This week, you will read about four of the times that Abraham's covenant was given. If you would like to read all of Abraham's story, read all of Genesis 12–25.

Read Genesis 12:1-9; 15:1-21; 17:1-21; 22:1-19.

DAY 1

1. Make a chart of God's promises to Abraham. List each promise on the side. Then place a check mark where each promise is recorded.

Promise	Genesis 12:1-9	Genesis 15:1-21	Genesis 17:1-21	Genesis 22:1-19

DAY 2

2. What did God repeat each time he talked to Abraham?

What did he add?

3. What does this tell you about God's response to continued worship and obedience?

DAY 3

4. What did it cost Abraham to worship God?

Day 4

5. What importance did God place on Abraham's worship?

6. God called Abraham to found a nation of God-worshipers—separate from others. Why would this have been difficult in Ur or Haran?

DAY 5

7. Circumcision separated Abraham and his descendants from non-covenant peoples. How does true worship separate you from non-believers?

8. What are your regrets about this separation?

9. How has God rewarded your trusting belief?

Pray, thanking God for calling *you* to worship him. Be honest in telling him about your regrets. Thank him for the rewards.

□ Week 29

Escape

Read again Genesis 15:13-14. God's prophecy came true. Abraham's grandson, Jacob, and his family of seventy went to Egypt to keep from starving during a famine in Canaan. Joseph saw that they were given good land in Egypt.

But a new king who didn't know Joseph came to power, and eventually the descendants of Abraham became slaves. They were forced to build the pyramids that still stand in that country.

Because there were so many Israelites now, the Egyptians began to be afraid and ordered the boy babies killed. But God spared Moses. The 400 years were almost finished, and he was ready to bring his people back to the land he had promised Abraham. Again they would be free to worship him.

Read Exodus 13:17–15:21.

DAY 1

1. What reasons can you give for God's leading the people across the sea rather than around it?

2. How was Moses' reaction to crisis different from his people's (14:10-14)?

DAY 2

3. In what specific ways did God protect his people?

4. What changes do you see in the people when you contrast 14:11-12 with 14:31?

DAY 3

5. Moses led his people in worship by singing a song to the Lord. Make a list of what he says God has done.

6. Make another list of his descriptions of God.

DAY 4

7. Now make a list of what God has done for you. Be specific—Moses was.

DAY 5

8. What characteristics of God do you enjoy?

Pray, praising and thanking God for these.

☐ Week 30

The Promised Land

Forty years have passed. Now the glory of God dwells in the ark of the covenant instead of in the pillar of fire and the cloud. Moses led his people right up to the border of the promised land. But they were afraid of the other tribes living there.

God did not force them to go in, but instead he made them wait in the wilderness until a new generation was born. Then, with only Caleb and Joshua remaining of the people who had crossed the Red Sea, the time again came to enter Canaan.

Read Joshua 3–4.

DAY 1

1. How was the experience of crossing the Jordan similar to crossing the Red Sea?

2. How was it different?

DAY 2

3. How did Joshua and his people show honor to God?

4. How did God bring glory to himself?

DAY 3

5. What was the purpose of the two piles of twelve stones?

DAY 4

6. Part of worship is telling our children of times when God has revealed his greatness to us. What kind of "stones" have your parents told you about?

7. What kind of "stones" are you setting up to help you and your children remember your own good times with God?

DAY 5

8. This week, create a craft object, painting, poem, or prose that will help you remember one of those victorious times. Write your plans or draw your sketch here.

□ Week 31

Punishment

Six centuries have passed. Israel, with God's help, has conquered the land of Canaan. But there has been a civil split. Now only the tribe of Judah even pretends interest in worshiping God. God gave them their promised land. He gave them judges, prophets, priests, and kings. Isaiah prophesied destruction because of the people's lack of pure worship. They had repented, and God spared Jerusalem from a vicious Assyrian invasion. But that was a hundred years ago, and the people have forgotten their repentance.

Now God sends the prophet Ezekiel, and, with the Babylonian armies bearing down, this time there will be no escape. Let's see what the religious leaders are doing.

Every Day

Pray every day this week for a different leader in your church. Pray especially that God will help that person grow spiritually and that he will protect him or her from false beliefs.

Day	*Name*
Monday	_____
Tuesday	_____
Wednesday	_____
Thursday	_____
Friday	_____

Read Ezekiel 8–11.

DAY 1

1. Read all of Ezekiel's vision (the four chapters) at one sitting. How does it make you feel about God?

DAY 2

2. Find four examples of false worship in chapter 8.

How were religious leaders involved in them?

DAY 3

3. What was the function of the man with the writing case?

4. In the upcoming battle, would God be on the side of the Babylonian army or the Judean army? Why?

DAY 4

5. Find evidence in these chapters of God's glory,

of his wrath,

and of his mercy.

DAY 5

6. What importance does God attach to the spiritual conditions of religious leaders?

□ Week 32

Back Home Again

About seventy years passed. The people of Judah were scattered, as God had said. Many died. Their city and temple were destroyed. But the Babylonian empire was nearing its end. King Cyrus of Persia conquered Babylon in 539 B.C., and Cyrus allowed what was left of the Jewish people to return to Jerusalem. A group of 42,360 came back. Had they repented? Were they quick to rebuild their temple and begin worshiping God again? After many years without religious liberty, what would they do with it now?

Nineteen years *after* their return, the prophet Haggai had something to say.

Read Haggai 1–2.

DAY 1

1. God spoke to his people through Haggai four times. When was each message given? What did each one contain?

Message #1:

Message #2:

Message #3:

Message #4:

DAY 2

2. What was the first concern of the people when they returned home?

3. What happened to their work? Why?

4. What does this tell you about God's power?

His interests?

His standards for his people?

DAY 3

5. God reminds the people of his promise (2:5). Read it again in Genesis 17:1-8 and Exodus 29:45-46. (The Exodus promise was given three months after crossing the Red Sea.) What methods had God used to keep his promise?

DAY 4

6. What value does God place on receiving true worship from his people?

7. What projects are you likely to put ahead of worshiping God?

DAY 5

8. What distractions are you letting hinder your worship?

As you pray today focus your mind on God. Ask his help in overcoming these obstacles.

□ Week 33

Confident Worship

The book of Hebrews was written to Jewish people who had become Christian believers. They loved their old faith—and their new one. Hebrews discusses the Jewish tradition and law and shows how Christianity grows out of it. This week we will study a small section that deals with right worship. If you want to learn more about this book that ties the two Testaments together, read Hebrews, beginning to end.

Read Hebrews 10:19-25.

DAY 1

1. What is the basis for our worship now?

2. How is our conscience an aid to worship?

DAY 2

3. What part do faith, hope, and love play in worship?

DAY 3

4. What responsibility do we have for each other as a part of worship?

DAY 4

5. What kind of encouragement do you need when you think of Christ's return (25)?

6. What kind of encouragement can you give someone else?

DAY 5

7. In view of the value that God places on worship, what attitudes about church attendance and personal devotions do you need to change?

8. Wrong attitudes are hard to change. Pray this week that God will help you with these; but you can begin his work by changing the related *actions* yourself. Write about one particular action that you will work on.

□ Week 34

Practical Advice on Worship

The apostle Paul was in prison at Rome. Soon he would be executed. No one had supported him at his trial. Most of his friends had left. Only the doctor, Luke, stayed with him.

Paul was concerned about all the churches he had started. They were full of new believers who were not used to distinguishing between true and false religion. And there were many false teachers. Would the believers become confused and stray away? Paul wrote to his young pastor friend, Timothy, with some final advice.

Read 2 Timothy 1–4.

DAY 1

1. Read the entire book at one sitting. Try to picture the writer. What do you see?

DAY 2

2. How does Paul build Timothy's confidence (1:3–2:13)?

DAY 3

3. What does he warn Timothy to avoid (2:14-26)? Why?

4. What characterizes false religion (1:14-19)?

Those who preach it?

Those they convert (3:1-9)?

DAY 4

5. What is Timothy's defense against false teaching (3:10-17)?

6. What special danger is there in teachers who tell you only what you want to hear (4:1-5)?

DAY 5

7. What false teachings have you been exposed to?

8. How are you building resistance against these?

Pray that God will keep you from being a weak person who succumbs to these teachings. Pray that he well help you seek out teachers who speak the truth, whether or not they make you feel comfortable.

☐ Week 35

Worship with the Psalms

The psalmists give us many examples of true worship. Select one of the psalms below for each day of next week. Read it several times. Meditate on it. Record answers to the questions. Use it as a prayer. (You may need to make minor wording changes as you pray the psalm.)

DAY 1

Read Psalm 25.

1. How does this psalm describe God?

2. What does it say about you?

3. What are you asking God to do?

4. What promises are you making to him?

DAY 2

Read Psalm 27.

1. How does this psalm describe God?

2. What does it say about you?

3. What are you asking God to do?

4. What promises are you making to him?

DAY 3

Read Psalm 34.

1. How does this psalm describe God?

2. What does it say about you?

3. What are you asking God to do?

4. What promises are you making to him?

DAY 4

Read Psalm 86.

1. How does this psalm describe God?

2 What does it say about you?

3. What are you asking God to do?

4. What promises are you making to him?

DAY 5

Read Psalm 103.

1. How does this psalm describe God?

2. What does it say about you?

3. What are you asking God to do?

4. What promises are you making to him?

E I G H T

Got the Message?
Live It Out!

If you've traveled this far in this studyguide, you've figured out that the Christian faith is no passive system of beliefs for eggheads huddled over their fine-print expositions of Greek and Hebrew texts. Sure, Christianity needs its scholars. But even scholars must eventually lift their heads (and their bodies) and go out into the real world. When they do, they find that Christian beliefs don't just rest in the brain. If they are beliefs at all, they touch every part of life.

We must live out these beliefs in the way we address a boss who makes sexually harassing remarks, in the way we respond to a neighbor who needs help—now—at the most inopportune time, in the way we react to ridicule when we talk about our faith and our audience rejects the message—along with the messenger. We must keep on keeping on in that faith, even if outward signs say, "You're a naïve, gullible chump; if your God is real, he certainly keeps himself in hiding."

During the next four weeks you'll look at some of the Scriptures that help us "live it out!" Whether you're a comfortable scholar or a hands-on performer, you'll find that faith in God, if it is real, will pervade all of life.

☐ Week 36

Faith during Hard Times

The setting is fifth century B.C., Judah. The Israelites had experienced spiritual revival under King Josiah. Now Josiah is dead and his two sons, in rapid succession, have become king. The people turned away from God. Furthermore, they were threatened by hostile empires around them: Egypt to the south, Babylon to the east. But the political threats didn't cause them to turn to God. Instead, the people seemed to be saying, "Grab it all now; it won't last long." In that latter phrase, they were terribly correct.

DAY 1

Read Habakkuk 1:1-4.

1. What is Habakkuk's complaint?

2. In view of his prayer, what would you expect to experience in Judah if you lived there?

3. What would you want God to do?

DAY 2

Read Habakkuk 1:5-11.

4. Do you think this is the kind of answer Habakkuk expected from God? Why, or why not?

5. How was life in Judah likely to change if God carried out this threat?

6. Why might it be hard to maintain faith in God during the crisis described here?

DAY 3

Read Habakkuk 1:12–2:1.

7. How might Habakkuk's description of God in this, his second prayer, help him endure the kind of trauma described in the previous section?

8. Write out three of the phrases Habakkuk uses here to describe God. Meditate on them for a few moments. (Try repeating them quietly several times as a praise to God.) If you truly believed that these words accurately describe God, how might they help you through a personal crisis?

9. Look again at Habakkuk 2:1. What does Habakkuk's plan of action suggest of his inner attitude toward God?

DAY 4

Read Habakkuk 2:2-20.

10. Notice the five repetitions of the phrase, "Woe to him . . ." (6, 9, 12, 15, 19). What had the people of Judah done that deserved these judgments?

11. What does this chapter say that confirms God's authority over all of life?

12. How would you feel if you were a prophet with this message?

DAY 5

Read Habakkuk 3:1-19.

13. What pictures come to your mind as Habakkuk describes the destruction he expects God to bring on his land?

14. How do even these word pictures of destruction inspire worship?

15. Read several times Habakkuk's words in verses 17-19. Why would it be hard for Habakkuk, knowing what he knows of the future, to pray these words?

16. How can his prayer become a model for your own faithfulness to God?

17. Try using the pattern of Habakkuk's prayer in verses 17-19 to make your own prayer of faithfulness to God. Substitute some of your own fears of tragedy for the fig tree buds and grapes on the vine of verse 17. Then pray Habakkuk's ending.

☐ Week 37

Repentance

Κing David was a "man after God's own heart." The New Testament describes him that way. But he would have also ranked high on any vice squad hit list. How can we reconcile the two? Are God's standards lower than those of the vice squad? No, they are infinitely higher. But God provides ways for relationship to continue, even when those he loves fall short of meeting those demands. God's moral standards are high. But if we fail to reach them, God invites repentance. It's his way of helping us to keep faith and live it out.

DAY 1

Read 2 Samuel 11:1-13.

1. What did David do wrong?

2. What complications arose out of that original wrong-doing?

DAY 2

Read 2 Samuel 11:14-27.

3. How did David compound his original sin?

4. What other people were affected by David's sin? How?

5. Read again the last statement of this chapter. In addition to the human losses resulting from David's sin, does God's displeasure seem to you a small or a large factor? Why?

DAY 3

Read 2 Samuel 12:1-25.

6. How did God demonstrate his hatred of David's sin?

7. How did David demonstrate his repentance?

8. What indications do you find that God still loved David?

DAY 4

Read Psalm 51.

9. How does David's prayer reflect a concern about his relationship with God?

10. What effects does he expect confession and forgiveness to have on that relationship?

DAY 5

Read Psalm 32.

11. What contrasts does David express in his condition before confession and forgiveness, and afterward?

Before	*After*
_____	_____
_____	_____
_____	_____
_____	_____
_____	_____
_____	_____

12. What responsibilities did David take on as a result of his restored relationship with God?

13. Read Psalm 139:23-24:

"Search me, O God, and know my heart;
test me and know my anxious thoughts.
See if there is any offensive way in me,
and lead me in the way everlasting."

Pray these verses. Now wait for God to bring sins to your mind. Ask his forgiveness and help in turning from these sins. Then believe that God has forgiven and cleansed you. Enjoy this, and express to God your thanksgiving.

☐ Week 38

Freedom and Responsibility

Right in the middle of an epistle whose theme is Christian freedom comes a little paragraph on responsibility. In the first few chapters of Galatians, the apostle Paul has been going on and on about not tying ourselves uselessly to laws, not putting unnecessary restrictions on our fellow Christians. "You were called to be *free,*" he says. Then, without taking a breath, he adds, now "serve one another."

From there he goes on to talk about the sinful nature. (We're supposed to fight it.) It seems that Christian freedom doesn't mean freedom to sin. And that leads to one of the loftiest statements in Scripture: a description of the fruit of the Spirit.

And all this in the context of freedom! Part of living out our faith means turning from sin (as David did), but also an inner growing of those nine God-breathed qualities: the fruits of the Spirit.

Every Day

Make a poster or large sign at the beginning of the week listing the nine fruits of the Spirit in Galatians 5:22-23. Each day for nine days, select a "fruit of the day." Write a definition for that fruit. Try in each situation you meet during the day to demonstrate that fruit.

DAY 1

Read Galatians 5:13-15.

1. How might an overemphasis on personal freedom pose a threat to Christian unity?

2. What problems have you caused people when you became obsessed with your own rights to freedom?

3. Talk to God about this. If it seems appropriate, take one step today toward healing those problems. Write your intention here.

DAY 2

Read Galatians 5:16-21.

4. What natural conflict does Paul outline?

5. What evidences in a person's life would indicate that the sinful nature is gaining control?

DAY 3

6. Which of the sins mentioned in verses 19-21 do you have little trouble with?

7. Which have plagued you in the last month?

8. Open yourself to God and ask him to enter your being and take over these areas still governed by your sinful nature. Our sinful nature has great power, so be ready to turn these areas over to him again tomorrow and next week. But perhaps by next month those sensitive areas will be less of a problem.

DAY 4

Read Galatians 5:22-25.

9. God does not take away our sinful nature and leave a vacuum. Instead he fills that void with the fruit of the Spirit. What opposites do you find in the list of the Spirit's fruit and the list of the acts of the sinful nature?

10. What benefits have you noticed as you have tried to live out this fruit?

DAY 5

Read again Galatians 5:13-26.

11. Notice especially the first and last verses of this section. How would obeying the instructions in between these verses improve relationships between Christians?

12. Bring to mind one relationship between you and another Christian or group of Christians that needs healing. What steps can you take to begin that healing by following the teachings of this passage?

Pray, asking God to cover that relationship with his own perfect nature and to allow you, even with your own imperfections, to be his instrument of reconciliation.

☐ Week 39

Reaching Out

Can we live the Christian faith in isolation? Can we read our Bibles, pray to God, attend our churches, work for Christian organizations, attend Christian schools, and in short, organize our lives in such a way that we avoid any intimate contact with non-Christians?

It sounds warm and loving and unstressful, but it falls short of scriptural commands in both Old and New Testaments. A necessary ingredient of the Christian faith is that it must reach out. It goes with the territory. A faith that locks itself in a religious ghetto is less than a full-blown, living, growing faith.

The prophet Jonah didn't like that aspect of God's plan. It's not that he minded sharing the faith, but he really preferred to choose his own audience. Something, however, went drastically wrong with that plan.

DAY 1

Read Jonah 1.

1. How were Jonah's purposes and God's purposes in conflict?

2. What could the sailors know about God from their experience with Jonah?

3. Look again at verse 17. If you had been Jonah in that situation, what would you have said to God?

DAY 2

Read Jonah 2.

4. What do you think was the purpose of the large fish?

5. What words and phrases here show that Jonah knew he was in trouble?

6. Look again at Jonah 1:1-3. What information in chapter two shows that Jonah had a change of heart?

DAY 3

Read Jonah 3.

Note: Nineveh was the capital city of Assyria, an enemy neighbor northeast of Israel.

7. What evidence do you see that Jonah did a thorough job of presenting God's message to Nineveh?

8. How did Nineveh exhibit repentance?

9. Do you think Jonah would be pleased or displeased with the results of his ministry? Why?

DAY 4

Read Jonah 4.

10. Why had Jonah at first refused to go to Nineveh?

11. Why was Jonah more concerned about the vine than he was about Nineveh?

12. How did God exhibit love both to Jonah and to Nineveh? (Draw your answers from the whole book.)

DAY 5

Read Matthew 28:16-20.

13. What similarities do you see between the job God gave to Jonah and the one he gives to New Testament believers?

14. How is this command from Jesus even bigger than Jonah's task?

15. What objections might today's Christians have to that job?

16. How might these two passages help you overcome your hesitations to live out your faith in a way that "makes disciples" for Jesus?

Beyond Mushroom Mentality

August 6, 1945. A mushroom cloud hovered over one city in Japan. Three days later, it happened again. And ever since that date every person alert to twentieth-century technology carries that same mushroom cloud in the back of the mind. On a moment's notice, it could hover over his or her own home. And life—if it continued— would never be the same.

Yet, more than a generation has passed since 1945. The mushroom cloud appears only on test sites—increasingly numerous. People who were children in 1945 have grown, married, birthed children, all the while wondering, "Is my baby the last generation? Or the next to last?"

Because they hear no answer, they put aside money for college knowing that the hundred-year-old college of their choice may vaporize next week. And life goes on—at its routine pace. So far, the mushroom cloud hovers only in the mind.

How should Christians deal with this uncertain future? We are not immune to its threat. Christians collect ulcers and colitis and migraines like the rest of the world's population. But though atomic warfare did not threaten the ancient world, the Scripture is not silent on the subject of an uncertain future. We can draw strength there, for God will teach us how to live, even under the threat of the mushroom cloud.

☐ Week 40

A Bleak Future

Suppose you've had the great fortune of getting in on the ground floor with the man who promises to be the biggest political giant of the decade. He was small potatoes when you first met him, but you see big things in the future. You quit your job, leave your family, pack a small suitcase, and spend two years as his aide. First you just follow him around, but soon he takes you into his confidence. He talks to the crowds in generalities, but for you he explains the deeper meanings behind his theories. You become friends. In time, even the crowds look to you as "one of the leaders." When the time comes, you know you'll ride into power with him.

Then disaster. Your mentor is arrested, convicted of crime, and executed—all in a matter of days. Your own future? Uncertain at best. And what little you can see doesn't look good.

It happened to the followers of Jesus. But even though he died, Jesus didn't leave them alone.

Read Luke 24 every day this week.

DAY 1

1. What uncertainties about the future did the followers of Jesus face?

2. If you could have listened in on the conversation described in verse 14, what phrases do you think you would have picked up?

3. Why do you think Jesus' followers did not recognize him at first?

DAY 2

4. What steps did Jesus take in revealing himself to them?

5. How might this slow recognition benefit these men?

DAY 3

6. Find as many references as you can to the Scriptures in this chapter. In what ways did Jesus emphasize the importance of Scripture?

7. What would it mean to the followers of Jesus that he opened their minds to understand the Scriptures?

8. In what ways has God opened your mind to the Scriptures?

9. What specific responsibilities do you think God gives you because of that increased understanding?

DAY 4

10. Look again at your answers to question 1. In what ways were Christ's actions a response to the uncertain feelings of his followers?

11. As they looked back at this crisis point in their faith, what touchstones would they claim as reasons to continue believing?

DAY 5

12. Read again verses 46-49. What responsibilities did Jesus give his followers?

13. How might this assignment decrease their apprehension about the future?

14. Read Luke 24 once more. As you review the way Jesus dealt with the fears of his followers about the future and the way he deals with your fears, what similarities can you find? Thank him for these.

□ Week 41

The Comforter with Us

When Jesus left his disciples and went back to his Father in heaven, he did not leave his followers alone, even then. He gave them the Holy Spirit—that person of the three-part God who lives inside all believers.

Many Christians feel a little uncertain about the Holy Spirit. It's unnerving to know that someone you can't see and don't know very well lives inside you. Then there's the whole area of Holy Spirit power. (Is it like a huge motor with no on-off switch?) And spiritual gifts. (Will I speak in tongues whether I want to or not?) Besides, the Bible doesn't say nearly as much about the Holy Spirit as it does about Jesus and the Father God. So we have every reason to feel uneasy about the Holy Spirit.

Yet, Jesus promised the Holy Spirit as a *Comforter* to help his followers through an uncertain future. In the age of the mushroom cloud, we need him more than ever.

DAY 1

Read Romans 8:1-17.

1. In your Bible, circle the phrase "Spirit of——" each time it appears. What do these names for the Holy Spirit tell about his character?

2. What reasons do you find here for letting the Holy Spirit invade your life?

3. Why might you hesitate to let God have that kind of control?

DAY 2

4. What does it mean to be God's child? (See verses 12-17.)

5. How do you feel about having this kind of relationship with Almighty God?

6. Talk to him about it.

DAY 3

Read Romans 8:18-27.

7. What evidence do you see around you that creation needs to be "liberated from its bondage to decay" (verse 21)?

8. What evidence do you see in human beings, that we too need that kind of liberation?

9. What is the nature of hope as it is described here?

10. In what ways does the Holy Spirit bring hope to a flawed world?

DAY 4

Read Romans 8:28-39.

11. Look closely at verse 28. Why might this promise help you face an uncertain future with confidence?

12. What conditions are attached to this promise?

13. Notice the sequence of five steps in verses 29-30. How might this add confidence to the hope already given by the Holy Spirit in verses 18-27?

14. Look again at verses 31-39. If you were worried that you were not quite good enough to stay in God's favor, how might these words help you?

DAY 5

Read again all of Romans 8.

15. Write a prayer to God the Holy Spirit expressing praise and thanks for the qualities described in this chapter.

16. If you were to wake some night in a cold sweat from a nightmare about the atomic future, what words from this chapter might bring you calming strength?

□ Week 42

Supporting Each Other

About a year after a new convert has become part of a group of Christians, he makes an astounding discovery: Christians are extraordinarily human. Sure, they are redeemed by Jesus Christ and tied to each other by the bond of his love. But they are also petty and jealous and selfish and, if pushed into a corner, may lie and cheat like anyone else.

The new convert takes a detached look at this motley crew he calls his "brothers and sisters in Christ," and calculates that he could live quite well without them. After all, God isn't limited to church buildings and fellowship groups. God can be found just as easily alone on a mountain top or in your own kitchen for that matter. Why endure the hassle of intimate friendships with Christians, who are otherwise so much like everyone else?

But the Christian faith is no Lone Ranger religion. Intrinsic to this faith is its group nature. Our new life in Christ demands fellowship. It demands living out through the give-and-take of community. It is that family of believers who form an insurance policy of protection against an uncertain future. Several passages of Scriptures speak to this. You'll look at some of them this week.

DAY 1

Read James 5:13-20.

1. Using the whole passage, in what ways are Christians to be responsible for one another?

2. What different circumstances mentioned here show the way a Christian's response is to be different from other people's?

3. Why are these responses best performed in a group setting?

DAY 2

4. In the drama of verses 14-15, what part does each person play?

5. What personality characteristics would an elder need to develop in order to perform this work?

6. What personality qualities would a person need to develop to receive this kind of help?

7. What protection do the instructions here offer a Christian who is tempted to stray from faith?

DAY 3

Read Romans 12:1-8.

8. What different meanings does Paul attach to the word *body* in these verses?

9. What effect does each of these meanings have on the way Christians function together?

DAY 4

10. Paul has told us that in the body of Christ, "each member belongs to all the others" (5). Using verses 6-8, contrast the way one might use each gift with and without an awareness of this truth.

Gift	How I might use it for my own benefit	How I might use it because it belongs to all the others
_____	_____	_____
_____	_____	_____
_____	_____	_____
_____	_____	_____
_____	_____	_____
_____	_____	_____
_____	_____	_____
_____	_____	_____

11. If you are to take to heart the words of verse 5, what changes should you make in your current relationships with people in your church or fellowship group?

DAY 5

Read Psalm 133.

12. What word pictures did David use to describe the unity of God's people?

13. What indications do you see that David considered this unity of great value?

14. If unity between God's people is, in part, an insurance policy for an uncertain future, what groundwork should you be laying now so that, if trouble comes, you can receive help from that policy? (Trouble might come in the form of social, emotional, spiritual, physical, as well as material needs.)

15. What groundwork should you be laying so that you can contribute to it when someone else is in need?

☐ Week 43

A Glorious Future

Suppose the worst happens. Suppose human beings manage to rise up and kill each other off and, at the same time, make the environment uninhabitable. What then? Is it all over? God's creation charred to nothing? God's people reduced to skeletons and piled alongside the rest? Is there any hope in this "worst case" future?

The last two chapters of the Bible say yes.

Read aloud all of Revelation 21–22 every day.

Every Day

1. Each day, tell God something different that you appreciate about the plan he has revealed in these chapters.

Monday

Tuesday

Wednesday

Thursday

Friday

DAY 1

2. How does this passage of Scripture make you feel? Why?

3. Find as many contrasts as you can between the new heaven and earth and what we have now.

Now   *Then*

_____   _____
_____   _____
_____   _____
_____   _____
_____   _____
_____   _____

DAY 2

4. What pictures of God's glory do you find in these chapters?

5. What do you see of his love for his people?

DAY 3

6. How will the relationship that God has with his people be different from what it is now?

7. Pray today, praising God for some of his qualities revealed in these two chapters.

DAY 4

8. What do you find in these two chapters that you will enjoy experiencing?

9. What connections do you find in the character of God, as it is revealed here, and what you have learned about him in your previous studies of Scripture?

DAY 5

Read Revelation 21–22 again.

10. What is uncertain about your own future?

11. What, according to these chapters, is certain?

12. How can the pictures presented here help you endure the uncertainties?

TEN

On-your-own Bible Study

> *O send thy Spirit, Lord,*
> *Now unto me,*
> *That he may touch mine eyes,*
> *And make me see:*
> *Show me the truth concealed*
> *Within the Word,*
> *And in thy Book revealed*
> *I see the Lord.**

You've been following a devotional guide for nearly a year now. You've formed consistent habits of Bible study and prayer. You've gathered ideas about what to look for in a passage of Scripture. You've learned to pray straight out to God or from his own prayer book, the Psalms. You've become aware that studying Scripture means change in yourself, and the change is sometimes painful. You are growing. But you can't forever follow a study guide. It's too limited—not aimed just at you. It's time to branch out and do your own study. You're ready for "on-your-own Bible study."

You deserve a mild warning, however. It's not easy. Those hidden meanings don't often leap off the page and scamper into your brain. Soul-searching questions that make you grow don't just happen. It takes work. But it's well worth the effort. And once you get used to studying the Bible seriously, it all comes rather naturally. This final chapter will teach you how to study the Bible inductively.

Inductive Bible study is a method of studying the Bible in much the same way that a scientist studies an unknown chemical. You first

* From "Break thou the Bread of Life," by Mary A. Lathbury, 1877.

read the passage as though you've never seen it before. (Maybe you haven't.) Then, through a series of regular steps, you discover its content and meaning.

During this two-month period, you'll have a chance to study nine passages inductively on your own. The steps of inductive study have been divided into six parts, one for each day. Read 1 Corinthians 15 and follow the study that is done for you. Then refer back to its example as you do your own study of the passages listed for each week. All quotes from the Bible are from the New International Version.

The first section using 1 Corinthians 15 is a sample. After that you'll find blank pages with an outline for your first week's work. For the remaining eight weeks, use a notebook to follow that same outline. But use the passages of Scripture listed in your studyguide. When you've finished that, you are truly "on your own." Happy exploring!

☐ 1 Corinthians 15

Sample Study

Day 1: First Glances

A. Once over lightly

1. What comes before?
A chapter about spiritual gifts, particularly tongues and prophecy.

2. After?
A final chapter of personal notes.

3. Author's style?
Logical, orderly.

4. How does it make you feel?
Encouraged, excited, important.

5. Major characters?
God, Christ, Paul the writer, believers.

6. Theme?
Life after death.

7. Conclusions?
God has conquered death. Keep on believing and working for God, because we will live forever with him. (56-58).

B. A closer look

1. Major divisions?
Verses 1-11, 12-19, 20-28, 29-34, 35-50, 51-58.

2. Illustrations?
If Christ was raised, then we also will be raised.

3. Order of events or teachings?
Christ was raised. That's why we believe in him. God has authority over all—even death. Our lives show that we believe Christ was raised. Our new bodies will be better than our old ones. The event of resurrection is described.

4. What can you know about the writer?
He was an apostle; he persecuted the church; he worked hard; Christ appeared to him; he felt unworthy (8-10); he lived in danger (30).

5. About the people he wrote to?
Believers who needed encouragement.

Day 2: The Big W's (and One H)

1. Who? Describe the characters and their relationships.
Brethren—Paul's readers
Christ—raised, was seen alive, firstfruits, the man of heaven
Cephas—saw the resurrected Christ
500 brethren—same
James—same
Apostles—same
Me (Paul)—Christ also appeared to him
God—has put all things in subjection
The dead—will be raised
Adam—First Adam became a living being; last Adam (Jesus) became a life-giving spirit
God's enemies—they will all be put under Christ's feet, last enemy to be destroyed is death
We—not all sleep, will be changed

2. What happened? List the sequence of events or progress of an idea.
Christ died, was buried, then raised. Many saw his resurrected body.
Therefore, God has conquered death and we, too, will be raised.

3. Where? Use a map. Check distance and geography.
Ephesus—Paul could have fought with beasts there. Corinth—
Across the Aegean Sea from Ephesus.

4. When? Tell when in history, time of day, year, or season.
Third day—Christ was raised.
"When he has done this, then the Son himself will be made subject
   to him who put everything under him" (28).
"When the perishable has been clothed with the imperishable and
   the mortal with immortality, then the saying that is written will
   come true: "Death has been swallowed up in victory" (54).

5. Why? Look for the words "because," "for," "when," "since."
"For since death came through a man, the resurrection of the dead
   comes also through a man" (21).
"For as in Adam all die, so in Christ all will be made alive" (22).
"For he must reign until he has put all his enemies under his feet" (25).
"For the perishable must clothe itself with the imperishable, and the
   mortal with immortality" (53).
"Therefore [because of this], my dear brothers, stand firm" (58).

6. How? Note by what process.
"In Christ all will be made alive. But each in his own turn" (22-23).

Day 3: Get the Picture

Studying the Bible can be like working a jigsaw puzzle. It takes a
long time if you just keep trying to fish pieces out of the box. Instead,
you lay all the pieces out, picture side up. Then you can see how it
fits together.

There are several ways to lay out the pieces of a Scripture passage.
Try *one* of the following on day 3.
1. Outline
2. Write a summary for each paragraph
3. Write your own paraphrase of the passage

4. Give a title to each paragraph

5. Draw a chart—see the chart for 1 Corinthians 15 on the next page.

Day 4: The Nitty-Gritty

One way to discover what a writer intended you to understand is to "get inside" his writing style and see how he put his words and concepts together. The Bible is excellent literature and will stand careful scrutiny. Look for the following elements of writing structure as you study a passage.

1. Repetition
Appeared—verses 5-8
Raised—verses 4, 12, 14, 16, 17, 20, 29, 32, 35, 43
Perishable-imperishable—verse 42, 50, 53-54
Sown—verses 42-44

2. Continuity—repeated use of similar terms
Raised/resurrection
Perishable/mortal
Imperishable/immortality
Fallen asleep/dead

3. Contrast—putting opposites side by side to emphasize their differences
Death came through a man, the resurrection . . . comes also through a man (21)
As in Adam all die, in Christ all will be made alive
Sown is perishable; raised is imperishable
Sown in dishonor; raised in glory
Sown in weakness; raised in power
Sown in physical body; raised a spiritual body
First man was of the dust of the earth, the second man from heaven (47)
Dead will be resurrected
Victory accompanies death

4. Comparison—putting similar things together for emphasis
I worked harder than all of them (10)

A body and a kernel of wheat (35-38)
The glory of a celestial body and the glory of a terrestrial body (40-41)
This glory is like resurrection (42)
First Adam became a living body, last Adam a life-giving spirit
As we have borne likeness of earthly man, so shall we bear likeness
   of the man from heaven (49)

5. General and particulars
I preached to you the gospel; then note the details of verses 3-11.

Paul's Argument for Life after Death (1 Corinthians 15)

Verse	Reason	Evidence	If it were not true . . .	Since it's true . . .
3-20	Jesus raised from the dead	He was seen by many	1) Our preaching and faith are in vain. 2) We are misrepresenting God. 3) You are still in your sins. 4) This life is all there is. The dead are dead forever.	Christ is the first of many who will be raised.
20-28	God has authority over everything, even death	Adam was God's creation. Yet all died because of his sin against God.	Some forces would be more powerful than God.	Everything—even death—is under subjection to God the Father.
29-34	Believers behave as if there is a resurrection.	Baptism. Their dangerous lives. They don't try to get all they can here.	The believers would eat, drink, and not risk their lives.	They must believe in a resurrection or they wouldn't live the way they do.
35-50	We will have new bodies.	In nature, seeds die and produce plants. As our first body was like Adam's, our second will be like Christ's.	Our current bodies wouldn't be suited for heaven.	God will prepare us for life with him.
51-58	Our resurrection will fulfill prophecy.	Isaiah 25:8 Hosea 13:14	We would be under the power of sin and law.	God gives us victory over death.

Day 5: More Nitty-Gritty

6. Cause and effect—Look for the words "then," "therefore," "since," and "because"

"If Christ has not been raised, then our preaching is in vain." (See the other if-thens of 12-19.)

"Therefore . . . stand firm" (58). This is the effect of all that Paul has said thus far.

7. Explanation—Look for the words "that," "so that," "in order that"

"So will it be with the resurrection of the dead" (42). (Then look back at 35-41 for the explanation.)

8. Introduction

"Now, brothers, I want to remind you" (1).

9. Progression—a sequence from least to greatest.

Christ died, was buried, raised, appeared (3-5)

If there is no resurrection, then (1) Christ was not raised; (2) our preaching is vain; (3) your faith is vain; (4) we are misrepresenting God; (5) you are still in your sins; (6) those who are dead have perished; (7) we all ought to be pitied (12-19)

Christ the firstfruits, then those who belong to him, then the end (23-24)

10. Questions—write the questions in the passage, then note their answers

"How can some of you say that there is no resurrection of the dead?" (12)

"What will those do who are baptized for the dead?" (29)

"If the dead are not raised at all, why are people baptized for them?" (29)

"Why do we endanger ourselves every hour?" (30)

"How are the dead raised?" (35)

"With what kind of body will they come?" (35)

"Where, O death, is your victory?" (55)

"Where, O death, is your sting?" (55)

Day 6: So What?

You have now completed a very thorough literary analysis of a portion of Scripture. If you had been studying a scene from Shakespeare, you would now be familiar with all its intricacies.

But don't stop. the Bible is not Shakespeare. It is a book to live by. What are you going to do with all the facts and understanding of the past week? God holds us responsible to act on this kind of knowledge. Ask yourself questions like these:

1. Do I believe this?
2. How should my actions show that I believe it?
3. How do I need to change my ideas? Values? Attitudes? Actions?
4. Does this answer a problem I am having?
5. What is God showing me about himself? About my relationship with him?
6. How can I worship God better because of this?
7. What does God want me to do?
8. What does he want me to become?
9. What is God promising me?

☐ Week 44

John 11:1-44

Day 1: First Glances

A. Once over lightly
1. What comes before?

2. After?

3. Author's style?

4. How does it make you feel?

5. Major characters?

6. Theme?

7. Conclusions?

B. A closer look
1. Major divisions?

2. Illustrations?

3. Order of events or teachings?

4. What can you know about the writer?

5. About the people he wrote to?

Day 2: The Big W's (and One H)

1. Who? Describe the characters and their relationships.

2. What happened? List the sequence of events or progress of an idea.

3. Where? Use a map. Check distance and geography.

4. When? Tell when in history, time of day, year, or season.

5. Why? Look for the words "because," "for," "when," "since."

6. How? Note by what process.

Day 3: Get the Picture

Use the next page to do one of the following:
1. Outline
2. Write a summary for each paragraph
3. Write your own paraphrase of the passage
4. Give a title to each paragraph
5. Draw a chart

Day 4: The Nitty-gritty

1. Repetition

2. Continuity—repeated use of similar terms

3. Contrast—putting opposites side by side to emphasize their difference

4. Comparison—putting similar things together for emphasis

5. General and particulars

Day 5: More Nitty-gritty

6. Cause and effect—look for the words "then," "therefore," "since," "because"

7. Explanation—look for the words "that," "so that," "in order that"

8. Introduction

9. Progression—a sequence from least to greatest

10. Questions—write the questions in the passage, then note their answers

Day 6: So What?

1. Do I believe this?

2. How should my actions show that I believe it?

3. How do I need to change my ideas?

Values?

Attitudes?

Actions?

4. Does this answer a problem I am having?

5. What is God showing me about himself?

About my relationship with him?

6. How can I worship God better because of this?

7. What does God want me to do?

8. What does he want me to become?

9. What is God promising me?

☐ Weeks 45-52

Now it's your turn. Use the six-day pattern for each of the following Scripture portions using a separate notebook for your Bible study. Not all the inductive questions will have answers in each passage. But keep digging. You'll be surprised at how much you'll find.

This unit has heavy emphasis on Bible study, but Bible study is only one part of a good devotional time. Don't forget to use part of your time talking to God. He speaks to you through his Word, and he wants you to speak to him in prayer.

Week 45: Matthew 7

Week 46: Colossians 1:1-23

Week 47: 1 Kings 18

Week 48: Joel 1—3

Week 49: Acts 2

Week 50: Psalm 8

Week 51: Proverbs 31

Week 52: 1 Corinthians 13

Prayer Notebook

I praise God because he is . . .   Date

I thank God for . . .   Date

Today I asked God . . .   Date of Request/Date of Answer

What God has shown me about himself today . . .   Date

Scripture Index